# Native American
## VECTOR MOTIFS

DOVER PUBLICATIONS, INC.
Mineola, New York

By Alan Weller.
Designed by Kerri Lakatos

The CD-ROM file names correspond to the images in the book. All of the artwork stored on the CD-ROM can be imported directly into a wide range of design and word-processing programs on either Windows or Macintosh platforms. In order to take full advantage of the unique capabilities of the vector format images you will need a vector-editing program such as Adobe Illustrator or CorelDRAW. As a bonus, we have included the freeware vector editor Inkscape on this CD. For more information, see the Read Me! file in the Inkscape folder on the CD. For the most up-to-date information about using the image files on this CD, please visit www.doverpublications.com/p991660.

ISBN 10: 0-486-99166-0
ISBN 13: 978-0-486-99166-5

Manufactured in the United States by Courier Corporation
9916651
www.doverpublications.com

# Native American
## VECTOR MOTIFS

001

002

003

004

005

006

007

008

4

009

010

011

012

013

014

015

016

017

018

019

020

021

022

023

024

025

026

027

028

029

030

7

031

032

033

034

035

036

037

038

039

040

041

042

043

044

045

046

047

048

049

050

051

052

053

054

055

056

057

058

11

059

060

061

062

063

064

065

066

067

068

069

070

071

072

073

074

075

076

077

078

079

080

14

081

082

083

084

085

086

087

088

089

090

091

092

093

16

094

095

096

097

098

099

100

101

102

103

104

105

106

107

108

109

110

111

112

113

114

19

115

116

117

118

119

120

121

20

122

123

124

125

126

127

128

129

130

131

132

133

134

135

136

137

139

138

140

141

142

23

143

144

145

146

147

148

149

150

151

152

154

153

155

156

157

158

159

160

161

162

26

163

164

165

166

167

168

169

170

171

172

173

174

175

176

177

178

179

180

181

182

183

184

185

186

187

188

189

190

191

192

193

194

195

196

197

198

199

200

201

202

203

204

205

206

207

208

209

210

211

213

212

214

215

216

217

218

219

220

221

222

223

224

225

226

227

228

36

229

230

231

232

233

234

37

235

236

237

238

239

240

241

242

243

244

245

246

247

248

39

249

250

251

252

253

254

255

256

257

258

259

260

261

41

262

263

264

265

266

267

268

269

270

271

272

273

274

278

275

276

277

279

280

281

282

283

284

285

286

287

288

289

291

290

292

293

294

295

296

297

298

299

47

300

301

302

303

304

305

306